Keto Bread and Keto Desserts Recipe Cookbook

All in 1 - Best Keto Bread, Keto Desserts, Keto Fat Bombs, Keto Cookies, Keto Snacks and Treats

(Healthy and Easy Recipes for Your Low Carb, Ketogenic, Gluten-Free and Paleo Diet)

By

Anna Bright

Legal Notice

ALL content herein represents the author's own experiences and opinions.

The information written, illustrated and presented in this book is for the purpose of entertainment only.

The author does not assume any liability for the use of or inability to use any or all of the information contained in this book and does not accept responsibility for any type of loss or damage that may be experienced by the user as the result of activities occurring from the use of any information in this book. Use the information at your own risk.

The author reserves the right to make changes, he or she deems required to future versions of the publication to maintain accuracy.

COPYRIGHT© 2019. All rights reserved.

TABLE OF CONTENTS

Introduction 1
Everything you should know about the ketogenic diet . 4
   The Ketogenic diet, concepts and benefits 4
   Benefits of the Ketogenic diet 5
   What to eat and what not to eat on a Ketogenic diet............... 8
   Foods to Avoid on a Ketogenic diet: 11
   Major types of gluten free Ketogenic flours.....................12
KETO BREAD RECIPES 15
   Recipe 1: Walnut bread 15
   Recipe 2: Pumpkin bread 18
   Recipe 3: Cinnamon bread 20
   Recipe 4: Gluten-free Garlic bread 22
   Recipe 5: Cashew Bread 24
   Recipe 6: Sweet Potato Bread 26
   Recipe 7: Flax Seed bread 28
   Recipe 8: Coconut flour bread with bacon 30
   Recipe 9: Blueberry bread 32
   Recipe 10: Almond flour Bread with olive 34

KETO FAT BOMBS 36
    Recipe 11: Keto Chocolate bombs 36
    Recipe 12: Coconut Keto bombs 39
    Recipe 13: Raspberry and cashew balls 41
    Recipe 14: Cocoa balls 43
    Recipe 15: Salted Macadamia Keto bombs 45
    Recipe 16: Almond butter cinnamon bars 47
    Recipe 17: Pistachio and Cocoa squares 49
    Recipe 18: Peppermint and chocolate Keto squares 51
    Recipe 19: Ginger patties 53
    Recipe 20: Blueberry fat bombs 55

KETO COOKIES AND MUFFINS 57
    Recipe 21: Pine Nut cookies 57
    Recipe 22: Almond Oreo cookies 60
    Recipe 23: Cocoa Keto cookies 63
    Recipe 24: Brownie cookies 65
    Recipe 25: Macadamia Cookies 68
    Recipe 26: Cocoa muffins 70
    Recipe 27: Keto Blueberry muffins 72
    Recipe 28: Pistachio muffins 74
    Recipe 29: Flax Seed muffins 76
    Recipe 30: Peanut butter muffins 78

KETO DESSERTS 80
    Recipe 31: Flourless chocolate cake 80

Recipe 32: Raspberry cake with white chocolate sauce.......... 83

Recipe 33: Ketogenic Lava cake 86

Recipe 34: Ketogenic Cheese Cake... 88

Recipe 35: Cake with whipped cream icing 91

Recipe 36: Walnut-Fruit cake 93

Recipe 37: Ginger cake 95

Recipe 38: Ketogenic orange Cake... 97

Recipe 39: Lemon cake 99

Recipe 40: Cinnamon cake.. 101

KETO SNACKS AND TREATS 104

Recipe 41: Ketogenic Madeleine 104

Recipe 42: Keto Waffles 107

Recipe 43: Ketogenic pretzels 110

Recipe 44: Cheesy Taco bites 112

Recipe 45: Nut squares 114

Recipe 46: Coconut snack bars 116

Recipe 47: Flax seed Crackers.. 118

Recipe 48: Almond flour crackers 120

Recipe 49: Keto sugar free candies 122

Recipe 50: Keto donuts 125

KETO SMOOTHIE, ICE CREAM, MOUSSE, MILKSHAKE, PUDDING 128

Recipe 51: Coconut milk Pear Shake...................................... 128

Recipe 52: Chocolate Pudding 130

Recipe 53: Raspberry smoothie 132
Recipe 54: Cocoa Mousse 134
Recipe 55: Coconut Ice Cream 136
CONCLUSION 138

INTRODUCTION

Welcome to this Ketogenic Cookbook that has been designed to help you kick-start your perfect Ketogenic journey and it will help you eat healthily, lose weight and at the same time still enjoy the mesmerising taste of guilt-free bread and desserts. You might wonder how that is possible to eat bread and desserts while you are on a Ketogenic diet and at the same time how you can keep your energy levels high.

Well, if you want to find an answer to the main secrets and learn how you can bake bread and make your favourite desserts, then all you have to do is to keep reading this cookbook because it will answer all your questions and it is the most perfect Ketogenic baking guide you have can find.. You might think that I am exaggerating, but once you start reading this cookbook you will discover that it offers you what many other books don't; this is the combination of some of your favourite ingredients like chocolate, strawberries, fruits and even candies, but all in a healthy way.

Whether you suffer from diabetes, from a liver disease, a kidney disease or you are just careful about your weight and don't want to gain any additional pounds, this cookbook is your heaven and haven. Yes, indeed, not only I am confident about what I have written for you because of my knowledge in this area, nor am I using a mere theoretical approach, but I am an experienced cook and I have a picked hand by hand all the ingredients I have used in the wide range of the recipes you will find in this book. I have chosen my recipes with great care to suit you all your needs.

Besides, with the help of this cookbook, you will be able to find the main basics of the Ketogenic diet, so that you can get an idea of how to get started on your Ketogenic diet and how to guarantee the success of this unique cooking style.

In this cookbook, you will also find a wide variety of recipes with pre-calculated nutritional information that will help you to govern your calorie intake. Moreover, you will learn and get to experience that adopting a Ketogenic diet can be an enjoyable experience more than an exhausting one, and you'll see with this cookbook that there is no need to feel deprived of your most delicious recipes.

So, if you are sick of trying boring recipes just because they include healthy gluten free ingredients and you want to change your Ketogenic experience for the better, don't hesitate to keep reading because you are on the right path. This cookbook will change all the conventional ideas you had about the Ketogenic diet and you will subsequently lose weight in less time than you expect.

I know you might have already tried and you might have failed, I had also tried many diets many times before trying the Ketogenic diet and I had failed. But I have finally succeeded with the Ketogenic diet and I myself experienced weight loss that I have wanted, I also managed to boost my immune system in no time. I didn't believe that I would lose weight until I saw it myself.

So, if you care about your health, it is the right time for you to challenge yourself and change your lifestyle once and forever. Get ready to make dreams into reality and learn some of the most delicious recipes you can ever try.

Adopting the Ketogenic diet will incredibly help you achieve weight loss, but it will also help you to relieve some of the most serious health conditions you might encounter like inflammation. Remember, the Ketogenic diet is not only a nutrition diet, but it is a mindset lifestyle.

In this book, you will find:

- The Ketogenic diet concepts and benefits
- What to eat and what not to eat on a Ketogenic diet
- A wide range of delicious recipes!

Everything You Should Know About the Ketogenic Diet

The Ketogenic diet, concepts and benefits

Congratulations on choosing the right path and taking the decision of following the Ketogenic diet and taking charge of your own health and of your entire lifestyle. But before moving forward to learn more about the Ketogenic diet, we should first focus on its concept and definition, so what is a Ketogenic diet?

The Ketogenic diet can be defined as a diet that is very low in carbohydrates and high in healthy fats. It may be surprising to you that the Ketogenic diet emphasises the use of fats to lose weight. Yes, indeed, using healthy fats is the cornerstone of the Ketogenic diet, mainly; because the high intake of healthy fats is an essential phase to make your body enter the metabolic state known as ketosis. But what is Ketosis?

Indeed, Ketosis takes place when our bodies use ketones to generate energy instead of using glucose and to obtain Ketones, we should use a high level of healthy fats rather than glucose. what is more important here is that Ketone bodies are usually derived from fats and not from glucose and once provided, ketones make a steadier source of energy compared to that generated by glucose. If you wonder why fats make a better source of energy compared to glucose, it is because glucose is derived from carbohydrates and usually ketosis takes about three to seven days to take place.

Since the Ketogenic diet is a low-carbohydrate diet, it provides moderate levels of high-quality proteins and high amounts of fats. This increase in the use of protein necessitates an adequate meal plan that may help you to stick to this healthy lifestyle-change.

So now that you have grasped and understood the basics of the Ketogenic diet, we should understand what makes a healthy Ketogenic meal? For instance, an ideal Ketogenic meal is made of about 10% of calorie intake from healthy sources of carbohydrates like dark leafy greens, berries, legumes, non-starchy vegetables. About 20% of the calories come from high-quality proteins like omega-3 packed fish, grass-fed proteins and about 70% of the calories come from fatty ingredients like avocado, nuts, coconut, seeds, and unsaturated and triglyceride oils.

Therefore, in a few words, maintaining an ideal Ketogenic lifestyle makes a great diet if you want to lose weight. Yet, more importantly, the Ketogenic diet is characterised by possessing a wide variety of health benefits. So, what are the major benefits and advantages of the Ketogenic diet?

Benefits of the Ketogenic diet

If you have recently adopted the Ketogenic diet or you want to go on a Ketogenic diet, but you are reluctant because you don't know so much about this diet or you are just wondering about the health benefits this diet may have, don't worry. Indeed, the Ketogenic diet has a massive health as well as therapeutic potential you might have never imagined. The benefits of the Ketogenic diet are not only various, but also unique. So, what are the major benefits of the Ketogenic diet?

For instance, the benefits of adopting a Ketogenic diet include important weight loss, a considerable increase in cognitive performance and more. Below is a list that explains the various advantages of the Ketogenic diet:

1. The Ketogenic diet plays a vital role in improving the cognitive function and abilities

Indeed, adopting the Ketogenic diet, the brain uses Ketone bodies coming from fats instead of glucose to generate energy. This can encourage stronger synaptic connection between the brain cells and thus can help the brain function better. If you are wondering what we mean by functions better, it means that the Ketogenic diet can increase mental alertness, it can make our mind sharper, and can improve all cognitive capabilities. Some studies have shown a great improvement in Autistic children who were following a Ketogenic diet.

2. The Ketogenic diet regulates the blood sugar

Studies have proven that the low-carbohydrate intake while following the Ketogenic diet may help improve the metabolism of insulin within our bodies and this is mainly because of the absence of carbohydrates from our meals. The Ketogenic diet can therefore, help our bodies maintain a balanced blood glucose level because it breaks down fats instead of glucose into ketones and turns them into energy.

3. The Ketogenic diet can help to lose weight

Believe it or not, the Ketogenic diet can help you lose weight in a short time. Not only do many clinical studies show the Ketogenic diet to support weight loss, but the Ketogenic is very well known for its role in suppressing appetite and reduce any cravings for sweets and starches.

4. The Ketogenic diet improves the Cardiovascular function

Studies have proven that the Ketogenic diet can help improve the metabolic health by using the energy from high-quality fats. This encourages weight-loss and transforms ketones from the high-quality fats into energy. Consequently, the Ketogenic diet can help you to have more balanced levels of cholesterol.

5. The Ketogenic diet can reduce the risk of seizures

It's believed that the combination of proteins with, fats and carbohydrates can considerably help our body use energy which results in ketosis. Ketosis can eventually lead to an important reduction in the seizures in people who suffer from epilepsy, especially in children.

NOTE:

So, if you are looking for a diet that can help you feel better and live healthier, the Ketogenic diet will be the perfect choice for you, but before starting with the Ketogenic diet, we should first learn what food we should eat and what food we should avoid. Can we still enjoy bread and desserts while we are on a Ketogenic diet?

What to eat and what not to eat on a Ketogenic diet

If you have recently adopted the Ketogenic diet for any other health reason; you should first learn more about this diet, including what to eat and what not to eat while adopting the Ketogenic diet. More importantly, you should have a clear idea on the ingredients you are going to use and the ones you must exclude from your daily meals.

Vegetable ingredients:

- Artichoke
- Asparagus
- Bamboo shoots
- Bean sprouts
- Bitter melon
- Bottle gourd
- Broccoli
- Brussels sprouts
- Cabbage (like bok Choy, nappa, green, Savoy or red cabbage)
- Cactus
- Cauliflower
- Celery
- Celery root
- Chayote
- Cucumber
- Eggplant
- Green or string beans
- Hearts of palm
- Jerusalem artichoke
- Jicama

- Kimchi
- Kohlrabi
- Leafy greens like arugula, collard, beet, dandelion, escarole, spinach, endive, watercress
- Leeks
- Mushrooms
- Okra
- Okra
- Onions (brown, red, green, scallions, shallot, white, spring, yellow)
- Pepper (jalapeño, bell, poblano, Sweet)
- Radishes (daikon, cherry belle, white icicle
- Rutabaga
- Sauerkraut
- Sea plants (dulse, arame, kombu, kelp, nori)
- Snow peas
- Sprouts
- Sugar snap peas
- Sugar snap peas, snow peas
- Summer squash (crookneck, delicata, spaghetti, yellow, zucchini, patty pan)
- Tomatoes
- Turnips
- Water chestnuts
- Watermelon

Herbs and spices:

- All fresh or dried spices like cardamom, chilli powder, curry, cinnamon, garlic powder, curry, ginger powder, onion powder, pepper, paprika
- Almond
- Blackstrap molasses
- Bone broth

- Bone broth
- Cacao nibs and powder
- Carob
- Fresh or dried herbs like dill, chives, basil, mint, cilantro, rosemary, oregano, thyme and sage
- Garlic
- Ginger
- Ginger
- Horseradish
- Hot sauce
- Hot sauce
- Lemon
- Lime
- Liquid amino acid
- Miso
- Mustard
- Organic apple cider vinegar, Vinegars, unsweetened
- Red wine vinegar white, red and balsamic vinegar
- Salsa, unsweetened
- Tamari/ Soy sauce
- Unsweetened Tomato sauce
- Vanilla

Allowed sweeteners:

- Luo han guo or monkfruit extract
- Stevia

Allowed beverages on a Ketogenic diet:

- Espresso/ Coffee
- Filtered water
- Green tea, rooibos tea (unsweetened)

- Herbal teas like mint tea, hibisicus tea and non-caffeinated herbal teas
- Mineral water
- Sparkling water

Foods to Avoid on a Ketogenic diet:

- All types of processed sauces and sugary foods are forbidden on a Ketogenic diet
- Smoothies like soda, fruit juices, ice cream, candies and grains are also not allowed on a Ketogenic diet
- Starches and grains are a big no-no in a Ketogenic diet, and particularly rice, cereal and pasta
- Most fruits except for limited amounts of berries
- Potatoes and carrots are not allowed
- Diet products and fats are not allowed
- Processed vegetable oils and unhealthy fats are to be such as processed vegetable oil
- All types of sugary alcoholic drinks like cocktails and sweet wines
- Sugar-free diet ingredients are also usually high in sugar
- Fast foods like burgers, pizza and pasta

Note:

Given the fact that the Ketogenic diet doesn't allow the use of sweeteners as well as grains and starches, you may feel confused as this book is centred on breads and desserts and you may wonder how that is possible? Well, the great surprise is that there are types of grain-free and gluten free flours that we can use even on a Ketogenic diet and the same applies to sweets and desserts. And to know more keep reading to discover the main types of flours you can use to bake your favourite breads.

Major types of gluten free Ketogenic flours

Low carb bread is known for being a healthier type of bread in comparison to regular bread and to bake Ketogenic bread, we need to provide several ingredients. The most used types of flour we use to replace wheat flour are almond flour, Psyllium husk powder.

- **Almond Flour**:

Almond flour is known for being one of the best substitutes for all-purpose flour conventionally used. Almond flour is known for being grain free and it is characterised by its low carb elements. It is recommended for Ketogenic followers. Besides, Almond flour is perfect for baking cookies, breads and snacks too. Almond flour possesses many nutritious health benefits.

- **Psyllium husk**

Psyllium is known for being a fibre made from the husks of the seeds of Plantago ovata plant. It is also known as Ispaghula. Psyllium husk is an ingredient that plays an important role in the alleviation of certain health issues like constipation. Indeed, Psyllium husk is known as a laxative; which signifies that it soaks up the water into your gut and then makes bowel movements easier for the body.

- **Coconut Flour:**

Coconut flour is a type of fine and soft flour extracted from the dried coconut meat. It is a known for being a product that belongs to the coconut milk products. Just like you can prepare your own coconut milk at home, you can prepare your coconut flour at home too and in your own kitchen. However, if you are seeking a quicker way to obtain coconut flour, you can just purchase it.

- **Flaxseed flour**

Flaxseed flour is a great alternative for all-purpose flour. Flaxseed is also characterized by its high content of fiber. Many studies have also proven that flaxseed can substitute eggs. Flaxseed flour is recommended for bread baking.

- **Sesame Flour**

Sesame flour is a gluten-free variety of flour that is extracted from sesame reduced-fat seeds. Sesame flour is usually white and fine, it is also rich in minerals. Sesame flour is also packed with vitamins too. Indeed, 75 grams of sesame provides the human body with its sufficient daily intake of magnesium, iron and zinc. It is also packed with Calcium and Vitamin E.

Sesame flour is also characterized by its high antioxidant propriety which makes is perfect to be used for bread.

Here are some abbreviations that may help you when baking a wide variety of your favourite recipes:

Abbreviations of general units

- 1 lb ....1 pound
- 1 oz ....1 ounce
- 1Tbsp 1tablespoon
- 1 Tsp 1teaspoon

The list of Nutrients use these abbreviations:

- 1 g ....1 gram
- 1 mg ....1 milligram

Keto Bread and Keto Desserts Recipe Cookbook

KETO BREAD RECIPES

Recipe 1: Walnut bread

Preparation time: 10 minutes

Cooking time: 35 minutes

Yield: 5-6 Servings

Ingredients:

- ½ Tbsp of butter
- ¼ Cup of chopped onion
- 4 Tbsps of chopped walnuts
- ¾ Cup of almond flour
- 4 Tbsps of coconut flour
- ½ teaspoon of baking soda
- ¼ Teaspoon of salt
- ¼ Teaspoon of nutmeg
- 2 Large organic eggs
- 4 Tbsps of beef broth

Directions

1. Start by preheating your oven to around 350 F.
2. Line a loaf tray with a parchment paper and set it aside. Meanwhile, melt the butter into a medium saucepan on a medium heat.
3. Add the onion and the walnuts to your saucepan.
4. Sauté the ingredients for around 2 to 3 minutes.
5. In a large bowl, combine the almond flour with the coconut flour, the baking soda, the salt, and the nutmeg and whisk very well.
6. Add the sautéed onion and the walnuts into your dry mixture with the eggs and the beef broth.

7. Whisk the mixture until it is perfectly combined.
8. Transfer your mixture into the already prepared loaf tray and then spread it evenly.
9. Bake the loaf of bread for around 35 minutes or insert a tooth pick to check if it is done.
10. Turn off the heat and remove your loaf from the oven and set it aside for 10 minutes.
11. Slice the bread; then serve and enjoy!

Nutrition Information

Calories: 90 | Fat: 6.8 g | Carbohydrates 3.8g | Fiber: 0.52 g |Protein: 5.3 g

Recipe 2: Pumpkin bread

Preparation time: 15 minutes

Cooking time: 65 minutes

Yield: 5 Servings

Ingredients:

- ¾ Cup of almond flour
- 2 to 3 egg whites
- 4 Tbsps of pumpkin puree
- 4 Tbsps of almond milk
- 2 Tbsps of Psyllium Husk powder
- 1Teaspoon of baking powder
- 1 Teaspoon of pumpkin spice
- ¼ Teaspoon of salt

Directions:

1. Preheat your oven to 345 F and then line a medium sized loaf pan with parchment paper.
2. Put a medium pan into the rack of your oven and pour water in that pan.
3. Combine your dry ingredients all together in a deep bowl and mix very well until it is perfectly incorporated.
4. Add the egg whites and the pumpkin puree to your dry mixture.
5. Pour the almond milk into the mixture and knead it until you form solid dough.
6. Knead the dough until it becomes dough smooth to the touch and place your dough into the loaf pan you have prepared.
7. Bake the pumpkin loaf in the Bain-marie for around 60 to 65 minutes.
8. When a toothpick you insert comes out clean, turn off the heat and remove your loaf pan from the oven.
9. Let the loaf bread rest for 15 minutes.
10. Slice and serve.
11. Enjoy your bread!

Nutrition Information

Calories: 75 | Fat: 4 g | Carbohydrates 2.5g | Fiber: 0.7 g |Protein: 3 g

Recipe 3: Cinnamon bread

Preparation time: 10 minutes

Cooking time: 45 minutes

Yield: 6 Servings

Ingredients:

- 1 and ½ cups of almond flour
- ¾ Teaspoon of baking soda
- ½ Teaspoon of baking powder
- ¼ Teaspoon of salt
- 1 Teaspoon of cinnamon
- ½ Teaspoon of ground all spice
- 4Tbsp of butter

- 2 Large organic eggs
- 1 Cup of avocado puree
- ½ Cup of heavy cream
- ½ Tbsp of grated lemon zest

Directions:

1. Preheat your oven to 340 F and line a loaf pan with parchment paper; then set it aside.
2. In a deep bowl, combine all together the baking powder, the salt, the lemon zest, the all spice and the cinnamon and mix very well.
3. Pour the butter in a bowl and with a hand mixer beat it until it becomes soft and very smooth.
4. Add in the eggs and the avocado puree then carry on mixing the ingredients.
5. Add your dry mixture and the heavy cream into your batter and mix it very well until it is very well combined.
6. Transfer your batter to your already prepared loaf pan then bake it for around 45 minutes.
7. After around 45 minutes, poke the bread with the knife.
8. Remove your bread from the oven and set it aside to cool on a rack.
9. Set the bread aside to cool down and after that, slice it.
10. Serve and enjoy it!

Nutrition Information

Calories: 173 | Fat: 15 g | Carbohydrates: 2g | Fiber: 2 g | Protein: 6 g

Recipe 4: Gluten-free Garlic bread

Preparation time: 8 minutes

Cooking time: 40 minutes

Yield: 4-5 Servings

Ingredients:

- 2 egg whites
- 1 and ¼ cups of boiling water
- 2 teaspoons of apple cider vinegar
- 1 Teaspoon of sea salt
- 2 Teaspoons of baking powder
- 5 Tbsps of ground Psyllium husk powder
- 1 and ¼ cups of almond flour

- For the Garlic butter: ½ Teaspoon of salt + 1 Minced garlic clove + 4 Oz of butter + 2 Tbsp of finely chopped parsley

Directions

1. Preheat your oven to around 360 F and then combine your dry ingredients into a deep and large mixing bowl.
2. Pour the boiling water; then add the egg whites and the vinegar to the bowl and keep whisking for around 1 minute, but make sure to not over mix.
3. With moist hands, form around 10 pieces.
4. Roll the 10 pieces into buns and then place them over a baking sheet.
5. Bake your buns for around 40 minutes in the oven. Meanwhile, prepare the garlic butter by mixing its ingredients and then refrigerate it.
6. Once your buns are ready, set it aside to cool for around 10 minutes.
7. Cut the buns into halves and then spread the butter on every half.
8. Raise the heat to around 425 F and then bake it for about 15 minutes.
9. Serve and enjoy!

Nutrition Information

Calories: 180 | Fat: 9 g | Carbohydrates: 12g | Fiber: 1 g | Protein: 5 g

Recipe 5: Cashew Bread

Preparation time: 10 minutes

Cooking time: 50 minutes

Yield: 6 Servings

Ingredients

- 2Tbsp of vegetable oil to grease your loaf pan
- 2 and ½ cups of whole raw cashews
- 7 Tbsp of coconut flour
- 8 Beaten large eggs
- ½ Cup of milk
- 4 Teaspoons of apple cider vinegar
- 4 teaspoons of baking powder
- 1 Teaspoon of salt

Directions:

1. Put a heatproof dish with around 2 inches of water and place it into the bottom rack of the oven and then preheat it to around 325 F.
2. Grease the loaf pan you are going to use and then line the pan with the parchment paper and press it to the bottom.
3. Set the dish aside and meanwhile, put all together the coconut flour, the cashews, the eggs, the milk, the apple cider vinegar, the salt and the baking powder and process the mixture for around 30 to 40 seconds.
4. Once the mixture becomes very thick, add 1 to 2 tbsp of water and process again until the mixture becomes smooth.
5. Transfer your batter to your already prepared loaf pan and bake it in the oven for 50 minutes.
6. Once the bread gets a brown color, remove it from the oven and discard it from the parchment paper.
7. Slice the bread; serve and enjoy it!

Nutrition Information

Calories: 183 | Fat: 13 g | Carbohydrates: 4.6g | Fiber: 2 g |Protein: 7 g

Recipe 6: Sweet Potato Bread

Preparation time: 15 minutes

Cooking time: 45 minutes

Yield: 5 Servings

Ingredients

- 1 large peeled and diced sweet potato
- 1 Tbsp of ground flaxseeds
- 3 Tbsp of water
- 2 and ½ cups of almond flour
- 1 Teaspoon of dried thyme
- 1 Teaspoon of fresh chopped rosemary
- ½ Teaspoon of sea salt

- 2 Tbsp of extra-virgin olive oil

Directions:

1. Preheat your oven to around 350 F.
2. Steam your sweet potatoes into a steamer basket in an instant pot or boil steam it in a steamer basket above the stove on top of boiling water for around 6 to 9 minutes.
3. Mix the flax seeds with water in a deep bowl and set it aside for around 10 minutes.
4. Mix again very well and mash the cooked potatoes with a potato masher or with a fork.
5. Add the rest of the ingredients and then add the rest of the ingredients and mix all the ingredients together very well.
6. Form the dough from your mixture and transfer your dough to a lined parchment and roll the dough with a rolling pin into around ½ inch of thickness.
7. Bake the dough for about 40 to 45 minutes.
8. Once the bread becomes brown, remove it from the oven and set it aside to cool down for around 20 minutes.
9. Cut the bread into rectangles.
10. Serve and enjoy!

Nutrition Information

Calories: 100 | Fat: 3 g | Carbohydrates: 11g | Fiber: 1 g | Protein: 4.9 g

Recipe 7: Flax Seed bread

Preparation time: 10 minutes

Cooking time: 30 minutes

Yield: 6 Servings

Ingredients

- 1 Teaspoon of salt
- 1/3 Cup of olive oil
- 2 Cups of flax seed meal
- ½ Cup of water
- 1 Tbsp of baking powder
- 2 Tbsp of maple syrup
- 4 to 5 beaten pasteurised eggs

Directions

1. Preheat the oven to around 350 F.
2. Line a 10*15 inch baking tray with parchment paper.
3. Whisk together your dry ingredients then add them to the wet ingredients to your dry ingredients and combine the mixture very well.
4. Set the batter aside for around 3 minutes until it thickens up.
5. Pour your batter into your already prepared tray and spread it into the bottom; but make sure to keep it away from sides of the pan.
6. Spread the batter into the shape of a rectangle for about 1 inch or 2 from the end of the pan.
7. Place the baking pan in the oven and bake it for around 30 minutes.
8. Once the bread gets brown, remove it from the oven and set it aside to cool down for around 5 minutes.
9. Slice the bread then serve and enjoy it!

Nutrition Information

Calories: 187 | Fat: 11 g | Carbohydrates: 7g | Fiber: 4g | Protein: 8 g

Recipe 8: Coconut flour bread with bacon

Preparation time: 11 minutes

Cooking time: 40 minutes

Yield: 4-5 Servings

Ingredients

- ½ Cup of chopped bacon
- 6 Medium organic eggs
- ½ Cup of butter
- ½ Cup of coconut flour
- ¼ Teaspoon of salt
- ¼ Teaspoon of baking soda
- 4 Tbsp of water

Directions:

1. Preheat your oven to around 390 F.
2. Line a loaf pan of your choice with a parchment paper and set it aside.
3. Melt the butter into a saucepan over a medium heat then set it aside to cool.
4. Crack your eggs then place them in a deep bowl.
5. Sift in the coconut flour; then add the salt, the baking soda, and the water into the same bowl and stir very well.
6. Toss the chopped bacon and then pour the melted butter into your mixture.
7. Whisk the ingredients until they become very well combined.
8. Transfer your mixture into the already prepared loaf pan.
9. Spread the mixture evenly and bake it for around 40 minutes into the oven.
10. Once the time is done, remove the loaf from the oven and discard its parchment paper.
11. Cut your loaf of bread into thin or thick slices.
12. Serve and enjoy your warm bread!

Nutrition Information

Calories: 235 | Fat: 23.6 g | Carbohydrates: 0.9g | Fiber: 0.8g |Protein: 7 g

Recipe 9: Blueberry bread

Preparation time: 9 minutes

Cooking time: 25 minutes

Yield: 6 Servings

Ingredients

- ½ Cup of cashew butter
- ¼ Cup of ghee, coconut oil or butter
- ½ Cup of almond flour
- ½ Teaspoon of salt
- 2 Teaspoons of baking powder
- ½ Cup of unsweetened almond milk
- 6 Beaten eggs

- ½ Cup of frozen wild blueberries

Directions:

1. Preheat your oven to around 350 F.
2. In a deep and large bowl, mix the cashew butter and the butter for around 30 seconds; then stir very well.
3. In a separate large bowl; combine the almond flour with the salt and the baking powder; then pour the cashew butter and keep whisking.
4. Mix the almond milk and the eggs; then pour it into the bowl and whisk.
5. Break your frozen blueberries and then gently stir it into your batter.
6. Line a medium loaf pan with a parchment paper and then lightly grease it with spray.
7. Pour the batter into your medium loaf pan and bake it for around 45 minutes.
8. Set the bread aside to cool for 20 minutes.
9. Slice the bread and toast it; then serve and enjoy it!

Nutrition Information

Calories: 160 | Fat: 12.8 g | Carbohydrates: 5.7g | Fiber: 1.1g |Protein: 6.9 g

Recipe 10: Almond flour Bread with olive

Preparation time: 20 minutes

Cooking time: 45 minutes

Yield: 5 Servings

Ingredients

- 2 Cups of golden flaxseed flour
- 5 Beaten egg whites
- 2 Yolks of egg
- 4 tbsps of olive oil
- 1 tbsp of baking powder
- 2 tbsps of apple cider vinegar
- 2 tbsps of Psyllium husk powder

- ½ Teaspoon of salt
- 6 Finely chopped sundried tomatoes
- ½ Cup of chopped black olives
- 1 Cup of feta cheese
- 1 Tbsp of dried oregano
- 1 Tbsp of dried thyme
- ½ Cup of boiling water

Directions

1. Preheat your oven to around 350 F.
2. Grease a small bread pan and line it with a parchment paper.
3. Combine the flaxseed, the baking powder and the Psyllium in a deep bowl.
4. Add the oil and the eggs and mix very well until you notice the mixture becoming like breadcrumbs.
5. Pour in the cider vinegar and combine the mixture; then add boiling water and keep stirring until your mixture starts to resemble dough.
6. Add the olives, the feta cheese and the dried tomato.
7. Pour your batter in the greased loaf pan.
8. Bake the bread loaf for about 45 minutes.
9. Slice the bread loaf; then serve and enjoy it!

Nutrition Information

Calories: 189 | Fat: 14 g | Carbohydrates: 8g | Fiber: 1.1g |Protein: 9 g

Anna Bright

KETO FAT BOMBS

Recipe 11: Keto Chocolate bombs

Preparation time: 30 minutes

Cooking time: 0 minutes

Yield: 12 Servings

Ingredients:

- 2 Cups of smooth peanut butter
- ¾ Cup coconut of flour
- ½ Cup of sticky sweetener
- 2 Cups of sugar-free chocolate chips

Directions:

1. Start by lining a large tray with a parchment paper and set it aside.
2. In a large mixing bowl, combine all your ingredients together except for the chocolate chips, and combine your ingredients very well until it is completely combined
3. If your batter is too thick or is crumbly, you may add a small quantity of milk or water
4. With both your hands, try forming small balls from the batter and arrange it over a the already prepared lined tray and freeze for about 10 minutes
5. While your peanut butter balls are in the freezer, melt the sugar-free chocolate chips in the microwave for about 30 seconds to about 1 minute
6. Remove the peanut butter from the freezer; then carefully and gently dip each of the balls into the melted chocolate
7. Repeat the same process until all the chocolate balls are covered in chocolate and arrange over a platter
8. Once you finish covering all the balls, place the balls in the refrigerator for about 20 minutes or just until the chocolate firms up
9. Serve and enjoy your delicious chocolate balls!

Anna Bright

Nutrition Information

Calories: 95| Fat: 9.7 g | Carbohydrates: 2.4g | Fiber: 1.2g |Protein: 3 g

Recipe 12: Coconut Keto bombs

Preparation time: 15 minutes

Cooking time: 0 minutes

Yield: 14 Servings

Ingredients:

- 1 and ½ cups of walnuts or any type of nuts of your choice
- ½ Cup of shredded coconut
- ¼ Cup of coconut butter + 1 additional tablespoon of extra coconut butter
- 2 Tablespoons of almond butter
- 2 Tablespoons of chia seeds
- 2 Tablespoons of flax meal
- 2 Tablespoons of hemp seeds

- 1 Teaspoon of cinnamon
- ½ Teaspoon of vanilla bean powder
- ¼ Teaspoon of kosher salt
- 2 Tablespoons of cacao nibs
- For the chocolate drizzle
- 1 Oz of unsweetened chocolate, chopped
- ½ Teaspoon of coconut oil

Directions:

1. In the mixing bowl of your food processor, combine the walnuts with the coconut butter; the almond butter, the chia seeds, the flax meal, the hemp seeds, the cinnamon, the vanilla bean powder, the shredded coconut and the chopped; then drizzle with the coconut oil.
2. Pulse your ingredients for about 1 to 2 minutes or until the mixture starts breaking down.
3. Keep processing your mixture until it starts to stick together; but just be careful not to over mix.
4. Add in the cacao nibs and pulse until your ingredients.
5. With a small cookie scoop or simply with a tablespoon, divide the mixture into pieces of equal size.
6. Use both your hands to toll the mixture into balls; then arrange it over a platter.
7. Store the balls in an airtight container or place it in the freezer for about 15 minutes.
8. Serve and enjoy your delicious balls!

Nutrition Information

Calories: 164| Fat: 14 g | Carbohydrates: 5.9g | Fiber: 2g |Protein: 4 g

Recipe 13: Raspberry and cashew balls

Preparation time: 15 minutes

Cooking time: 0 minutes

Yield: 14 Servings

Ingredients:

- 1⅓ Cup of raw cashews or almonds
- ¼ Cup of cashew or almond butter
- 2 Tablespoons of coconut oil
- 2 Pitted Medjool dates, pre-soaked into hot water for about 10 minutes
- ½ Teaspoon of vanilla extract
- ¼ Teaspoon of kosher salt

- ½ Cup of freeze-dried and lightly crashed raspberries
- ⅓ Cup of chopped dark chocolate

Directions:

1. In a high-powered blender or a Vitamix; combine the cashews or almonds with the butter, the coconut oil, the Medjool dates, the vanilla extract and the salt and pulse on a high speed for about 1 to 2 minutes or until the batter starts sticking together.
2. Pulse in the dried raspberries and the dark chocolate until your get a thick mixture.
3. With a tablespoon or a small cookie scoop, divide the mixture into balls of equal size.
4. Arrange the balls in a container or a zip-top bag in a refrigerator for about 2 weeks or just serve and enjoy your delicious cashew balls!

Nutrition Information

Calories: 108.2| Fat: 7.4 g | Carbohydrates: 5.9g | Fiber: 1.3g |Protein: 3 g

Recipe 14: Cocoa balls

Preparation time: 90 minutes

Cooking time: 0 minutes

Yield: 9 Servings

Ingredients:

- 1 Cup of almond butter
- 1 Cup of coconut oil, at room temperature
- ½ Cup of unsweetened cocoa powder
- 1/3 Cup of coconut flour
- ¼ Teaspoon of powdered stevia
- 1/16 tsp of pink Himalayan salt

Directions:

1. In a small pot and over a medium high heat, melt the almond butter and combine it with the coconut oil.
2. Add the coconut flour, the cocoa powder and the Himalayan salt and stir.
3. Add the stevia and mix again; then let your mixture cool.
4. Pour the mixture in a large bowl and transfer it to the freezer to solidify for about 60 to 90 minutes.
5. Once solidified, remove the bowl from the freezer and form it into balls.
6. Form balls from the batter and arrange the balls over a tray lined with a parchment paper.
7. Refrigerate the balls for about 15 minutes.
8. Serve and enjoy your delicious Ketogenic bombs!

Nutrition Information

Calories: 157| Fat: 12.6 g | Carbohydrates: 3.4g | Fiber: 1.8g |Protein: 3.7 g

Recipe 15: Salted Macadamia Keto bombs

Preparation time: 35 minutes

Cooking time: 0 minutes

Yield: 12 Servings

Ingredients:

- 10 Tablespoons of Coconut Oil
- 5 Tablespoons of Unsweetened Cocoa Powder
- 1 Tablespoon of Granulated Stevia
- 3 Tablespoon of coarsely chopped Macadamia Nuts
- 1 Pinch of Coarse Sea Salt to taste

Directions:

1. Melt the coconut oil over the stove.
2. Add the cocoa powder and the granulated Stevia.
3. Mix your ingredients and remove it from the heat.
4. Spoon the mixture into silicone candy moulds until the mould is about ¾ full.
5. Refrigerate the moulds for about 5 minutes.
6. Sprinkle the macadamia nut in each of the silicone moulds and press down; then return the moulds to the refrigerator and let cool for about 30 minutes.
7. Sprinkle macadamia nuts into each well. Press down to distribute the nuts.
8. Once the chocolates are cool and set, remove it from the refrigerator; then let sit at room temperature and sprinkle with coarse salt.
9. Serve and enjoy your delicious macadamia salted balls!

Nutrition Information

Calories: 120| Fat: 13 g | Carbohydrates: 3g | Fiber: 1.3g |Protein: 2.5 g

Recipe 16: Almond butter cinnamon bars

Preparation time: 35 minutes

Cooking time: 0 minutes

Yield: 15 Servings

Ingredients:

- ½ Cup of creamed coconut, chopped into chunks
- 1/8 Teaspoon of ground cinnamon

For the first Icing:

- 1 Tablespoon of non-melted extra virgin coconut oil
- 1 Tablespoon of almond butter

For the Second Icing:

- 1 Tablespoon of extra virgin almond butter
- ½ Teaspoon of ground cinnamon

Directions:

1. Start by lining a muffin pan with muffin liners.
2. In a large mixing bowl and using both your hands, combine the coconut cream with cinnamon and mix very well.
3. Pat the mixture into the dish; make sure to fill 2 mini loaf sections.
4. Then prepare the first icing by whisking the coconut oil with the almond butter and spread the mixture over the creamed coconut.
5. Put the bars into the freezer for about 6 minutes.
6. In the meantime, prepare the second Icing by whisking the icing almond butter with the cinnamon and drizzle it on top of the bars.
7. Place the bars in the refrigerator for about 30 minutes or for about 8 minutes in the freezer.
8. Cut the frozen batter into bars with a knife.
9. Serve and enjoy your delicious bars!

Nutrition Information

Calories: 160| Fat: 7 g | Carbohydrates: 18g | Fiber: 1g |Protein: 3.2 g

Recipe 17: Pistachio and Cocoa squares

Preparation time: 25 minutes

Cooking time: 5 minutes

Yield: 13 Servings

Ingredients:

- ½ Cup of finely chopped and cacao butter
- 1 Cup of roasted almond butter
- 1 Cup of creamy coconut butter
- 1 Cup of firm coconut oil
- ½ Cup of full fat coconut milk, chilled for an overnight
- ¼ Cup of ghee

- 1 Tablespoon of pure vanilla extract
- 2 Teaspoons of chai spice
- ¼ Teaspoon of pure almond extract
- ¼ Teaspoon of Himalayan salt
- ¼ Cup of chopped raw pistachios, shelled

Directions:

1. Grease a square baking pan of about 9" sand line it with a parchment paper; make sure to leave a little bit hanging on both sides to help you unmold easily; then set aside.
2. Melt the cacao butter in the oven for about 30 seconds and reserve it.
3. Add the roasted almonds, the coconut butter, the coconut oil, the coconut milk, the ghee, the vanilla extract, the spice, the almond extract, the salt and the chopped pistachios to a large mixing bowl and mix very well starting with a low speed; then increase the speed and mix until the mixture become airy.
4. Pour the mixed and melted cacao butter into that of the almond and keep mixing on a high speed until you get an incorporated batter.
5. Transfer the prepared pan; then evenly spread the batter and sprinkle with the chopped pistachios.
6. Refrigerate your batter for about 4 hours or for an overnight.
7. Cut into about 36 squares; then serve and enjoy!

Nutrition Information

Calories: 170| Fat: 17 g | Carbohydrates: 3.1g | Fiber: 1.5g |Protein: 2.4 g

Recipe 18: Peppermint and chocolate Keto squares

Preparation time: 10 minutes

Cooking time: 0 minutes

Yield: 10 Servings

Ingredients:

For the peppermint filling:

- ½ Cup of coconut butter
- 1 Tablespoon of melted coconut oil
- 1 Teaspoon of peppermint extract

- 2 Tablespoons of Stevia

For the chocolate layer:

- 2 Tablespoons of melted coconut oil
- 4 Oz of 100% dark chocolate

Directions:

1. In a large mixing bowl, combine all together the coconut butter with the melted coconut oil, the peppermint extract and the stevia and mix very well.
2. Pour a small quantity of peppermint mixture into silicone muffin trays to form a layer of about 1/3 inch of thickness.
3. Freeze for about 1 hour; then melt the dark chocolate with the coconut oil and mix again.
4. Remove the firm peppermint filling from the cups.
5. Pour a small quantity of the chocolate mixture into each of the cups in a way that it covers the base; then cover with more chocolate.
6. Repeat the same process with the remaining cups.
7. Let the patties cool for about 2 hours until it becomes solid; then let thaw for about 10 minutes.
8. Serve and enjoy your patties!

Nutrition Information

Calories: 153| Fat: 13 g | Carbohydrates: 3g | Fiber: 2g |Protein: 4 g

Recipe 19: Ginger patties

Preparation time: 10 minutes

Cooking time: 0 minutes

Yield: 15 Servings

Ingredients:

- 1 Cup of coconut butter, softened
- 1 Cup of coconut oil, softened
- ½ Cup of shredded coconut; unsweetened
- 1 Teaspoon of stevia
- 1 Teaspoon of ginger powder

Directions:

1. Mix the softened coconut butter with the coconut oil, the stevia, the shredded coconut and the ginger powder and mix very well until your ingredients are very well dissolved.
2. Pour the batter into the silicon moulds and refrigerate for about 10 minutes.
3. Serve and enjoy your ginger patties.

Nutrition Information

Calories: 123| Fat: 12.7 g | Carbohydrates: 2.4g | Fiber: 1.2g |Protein: 1.8 g

Recipe 20: Blueberry fat bombs

Preparation time: 5 minutes

Cooking time: 0 minutes

Yield: 30 Servings

Ingredients:

- 4 Oz of soft goat's cheese
- ½ Cup of fresh blueberries
- 1 Cup of almond flour
- 1 Teaspoon of vanilla extract
- ½ Cup of pecans
- ½ Teaspoon of stevia
- ¼ Cup of unsweetened shredded coconut

Directions:

1. Process the goat cheese with the fresh blueberries, the almond flour, the vanilla extract, the pecans, the stevia and the unsweetened shredded coconut in a food processor and process very well
2. Roll the mixture into about 30 small fat bombs
3. Pour the coconut flakes in a bowl and lightly roll each of the fat bombs into the shredded coconut
4. Serve and enjoy your delicious fat bombs!

Nutrition Information

Calories: 49| Fat: 5 g | Carbohydrates: 1g | Fiber: 1g |Protein: 2.3 g

Keto Bread and Keto Desserts Recipe Cookbook

KETO COOKIES AND MUFFINS

Recipe 21: Pine Nut cookies

Preparation time: 10 minutes

Cooking time: 12 minutes

Yield: 20 Servings

Ingredients:

- 1 Large egg
- 1 Teaspoon of almond extract
- 1 Pinch of salt
- 1 Cup of stevia
- 2 Cups of superfine blanched almond flour
- 1/3 Cup of pine nuts

Directions:

1. Preheat your oven to a temperature of about 325 degrees Fahrenheit.
2. Mix the eggs with the almond extract, the salt and the sweetener in a bowl of a medium.
3. Beat your ingredients with a mixer for about 2 minutes or until the mixture becomes glossy.
4. Add in the almond flour and beat your ingredients until it becomes fluffy.
5. If the dough gets too dry, add about tablespoon of water in a way that it holds up very well together.
6. Place the nuts over a small platter.
7. Take a pinch of the dough and roll it into one piece of about 1 inch in its diameter.
8. Press the top of the ball dough into the nut with the side up.
9. Place the cookie over a parchment paper lined cookie sheet lined with a parchment paper.
10. Repeat the same process with the remaining dough; you can get about 20 cookies.
11. Bake your cookies in the oven for about 12 minutes.
12. Remove the cookies from the oven and let cool for about 6 minutes.
13. Serve and enjoy your cookies.

Nutrition Information

Calories: 83| Fat: 7.5 g | Carbohydrates: 2.4g | Fiber: 1g |Protein: 4 g

Recipe 22: Almond Oreo cookies

Preparation time: 15 minutes

Cooking time: 12 minutes

Yield: 25 Servings

Ingredients:

- 2 and ¼ cups of hazelnut or almond flour
- 3 Tablespoons of coconut flour
- 4 Tablespoons of cocoa powder
- 1 Teaspoons of baking powder

- ½ Teaspoon of xanthan gum
- ¼ Teaspoon of salt
- ½ Cup of softened butter
- ½ Cup of stevia
- 1 Large egg
- 1 Teaspoon of vanilla extract

For the Cream Filling:

- 4 Oz of softened cream cheese
- 2 Tablespoons of almond butter
- ½ Teaspoons of pure vanilla extract
- ½ Cup of powdered of Swerve, you can just grind it in a spice grinder

Directions:

1. Preheat your oven to a temperature of about 350 degrees Fahrenheit.
2. Combine the hazelnut or the almond flour with the cocoa powder, the baking powder, the xanthan gum, the salt, the stevia, the egg and the vanilla extract in a large bowl and mix very well.
3. Add the almond butter and mix again.
4. In a separate medium bowl, cream all together the Swerve and the butter until it become light and extremely fluffy for 2 to 3 minutes.
5. Add the egg and the vanilla and mix until your ingredients are fully combined.
6. Add your already mixed dry ingredients and mix it until it is very well combined.
7. Roll out the obtained dough between two rectangular waxed paper sheets; make sure the thickness is about 1/8.

8. Place the dough over a cookie sheet lined with a parchment paper.
9. Roll the cookie dough again until the end.
10. Bake the cookies for about 12 minutes; then let cool completely before starting to fill.

To make the filling:
11. Cream the cream cheese with the butter; then cream all together and add the vanilla extract.
12. Gradually add in the powdered swerve.
13. Fill the Oreo cookies with the cream.
14. Serve and enjoy your delicious cookies!

Nutrition Information

Calories: 136| Fat: 12.3 g | Carbohydrates: 2.8g | Fiber: 1.8g |Protein: 4.6 g

Recipe 23: Cocoa Keto cookies

Preparation time: 10 minutes

Cooking time: 15 minutes

Yield: 11 Servings

Ingredients:

- ½ Cup of Swerve confectioner
- ½ Cup of Unsweetened Cocoa Powder
- 4 Tablespoons of almond butter
- 2 Large Eggs
- 1 Teaspoon of vanilla extract
- 1 Cup of Almond Flour
- 1 Teaspoon of baking powder

- 1 Pinch of Pink Salt

Directions:

1. Combine the cocoa powder with the swerve in a large mixing bowl; then add then add the melted butter to the mixture and combine all together with the help of a hand mixer.
2. Once your ingredients are very well combined, add the eggs, the vanilla, and the baking powder and mix again.
3. Add in the almond flour and mix again; the batter should be thick.
4. Form cookies from the dough and arrange it over a baking sheet.
5. Bake your cookies for about 13 to 14 minutes at a temperature if about 350 F.
6. Serve and enjoy your cookies or store them in a clean container to serve whenever you want!

Nutrition Information

Calories: 168| Fat: 17.4 g | Carbohydrates: 2.5g | Fiber: 1g |Protein: 4

Recipe 24: Brownie cookies

Preparation time: 20 minutes

Cooking time: 10 minutes

Yield: 11 Servings

Ingredients:

- 2 Tablespoons of softened almond butter
- 1 Large egg
- 1 Tablespoon of Truvia
- ¼ Cup of Splenda
- 1/8 Teaspoon of blackstrap molasses
- 1 Tablespoon of vita fiber syrup
- 1 Teaspoon of vanilla extract
- 6 Tablespoon of sugar-free chocolate-chips

- 1 Teaspoon of almond butter
- 6 Tablespoons of almond flour
- 1 Tablespoon of cocoa powder
- 1/8 Teaspoon of baking powder
- 1/8 Teaspoon of salt
- ¼ Teaspoon of xanthan gum
- ¼ Cup of chopped pecans
- 1 Tablespoon of sugar-free chocolate-chips

Directions:

1. In a medium bowl, and with a hand mixer, mix all together two tablespoons of almond butter with the egg, the sweeteners, the vita fiber and the vanilla and combine for about 2 minutes.
2. In a separate medium bowl, microwave the chocolate chips and about 1 tablespoon of the almond butter for about 30 seconds.
3. Beat the chocolate into the mixture of eggs and butter and mix until you get a smooth batter.
4. Stir in the remaining almond flour, the cocoa powder, the baking powder, the salt, the xanthan gum, the chopped pecans and the chocolate chips.
5. Place the batter in the freezer for about 7 to 8 minutes to firm up; then preheat your oven to about 350 F.
6. Spray a large baking sheet with oil and make the shape of cookies with your hands.
7. Arrange the cookies over the baking sheet and lightly flatten each of the cookies with your hand or with the back of an oiled spoon.
8. Bake your cookies for about 8 to 10min.
9. Let the cookies rest for about 10 minutes to cool.
10. Serve and enjoy your delicious cookies!

Nutrition Information

Calories: 61| Fat: 4 g | Carbohydrates: 6g | Fiber: 0.9g |Protein: 1.2

Recipe 25: Macadamia Cookies

Preparation time: 20 minutes

Cooking time: 10 minutes

Yield: 11 Servings

Ingredients:

- 1/2 cup coconut oil, melted
- 2 tablespoons almond butter
- 1 egg
- 1 1/2 cup almond flour
- 2 tablespoons unsweetened cocoa powder
- 1/2 cup granulated erythritol sweetener
- 1 teaspoon vanilla extract
- 1/2 teaspoon baking soda
- 1/4 cup chopped macadamia nuts

- 1 Pinch of salt

Directions:

1. Start by preheating your oven to a temperature of about 350 F.
2. Combine the almond butter with the coconut oil, the almond flour, the cocoa powder, the swerve, the vanilla extract, the baking soda, the chopped macadamia nut and the salt in a large mixing bowl.
3. Mix your ingredients very well with a fork or a spoon; then set it aside.
4. Line a cookie sheet with a parchment paper or just grease it very well.
5. Drop small balls of about 1 ½ inches wide; then gently flatten the cookies with your hands.
6. Bake your cookies for about 15 minutes; then remove them from the oven and set them aside to cool for about 10 minutes.
7. Serve and enjoy your cookies!

Nutrition Information

Calories: 179| Fat: 17 g | Carbohydrates: 4g | Fiber: 2g |Protein: 5

Recipe 26: Cocoa muffins

Preparation time: 10 minutes

Cooking time: 20 minutes

Yield: 12 Servings

Ingredients:

1. 1 ¼ Cups of Almond Flour
2. ½ Cup of cocoa powder, unsweetened Cocoa Powder
3. ½ cup of Erythritol
4. 1 and ½ Teaspoons of Baking Powder
5. 1 teaspoon of pure Vanilla Extract
6. 3 Large eggs
7. 2/3 Cup of heavy Cream
8. 3 Ounces of melted almond butter
9. ½ Cup of Chocolate Chips; Sugar-Free

Directions:

1. Preheat your oven to a temperature of about 350 F.
2. In a large bowl, combine the almond flour with the cocoa powder, the erythritol and the baking powder and mix very well
3. Add in the vanilla extract, the eggs, and the heavy cream and mix very well.
4. Add in the melted coconut oil and mix again
5. Add in the sugar-free chocolate chips to your ingredients and stir very well.
6. Line a muffin tray with cupcake papers
7. Spoon your prepared mixture into the 12 holes of a standard muffin tray or any muffin tray you have
8. Bake your muffins for about 20 minutes
9. Remove the muffins from the oven and let cool for 5 minutes
10. Serve and enjoy your delicious muffins!

Nutrition Information

Calories: 304| Fat: 23 g | Carbohydrates: 9g | Fiber: 2g |Protein: 7

Recipe 27: Keto Blueberry muffins

Preparation time: 8 minutes

Cooking time: 25 minutes

Yield: 12 Servings

Ingredients:

- 2 and ½ cups of blanched almond flour
- ½ Cup of Erythritol
- 1 and ½ teaspoons of Gluten-free baking powder
- ¼ Teaspoon of Sea salt
- 1/3 Cup of Coconut oil
- 1/3 Cup of Unsweetened almond milk
- 3 large Eggs
- ½ Teaspoon of Vanilla extract
- ¾ Cup of Blueberries

Directions:

1. Preheat your oven to a temperature of about 350 F.
2. Line a standard muffin tray with 12 parchment muffin liners.
3. In a large bowl, stir all together the erythritol with the baking powder and the sea salt.
4. Mix in the coconut oil; the almond milk, the eggs and the vanilla extract.
5. Add in the blueberries; then equally distribute the batter among the muffin cups.
6. Bake your muffins for about 20 to 25 minutes.
7. Serve and enjoy your sumptuous muffins!

Nutrition Information

Calories: 217| Fat: 19 g | Carbohydrates: 6g | Fiber: 3g |Protein: 8

Recipe 28: Pistachio muffins

Preparation time: 10 minutes

Cooking time: 30 minutes

Yield: 12 Servings

Ingredients:

- 4 Large Eggs, it is better to use brown Eggs
- ½ Cup of almond butter, unsalted
- ¼ Cup of confectioners Swerve
- ¼ Cup of Organic Stevia Blend by Pyure
- 1 Teaspoon of Pistachio Extract
- ½ Cup of Almond Milk, unsweetened
- 1 Teaspoon of Vanilla Extract
- 1 Cup of blanched Almond Flour
- ½ Cup of Organic Coconut Flour

- 2 Teaspoons of Baking Powder
- ½ Teaspoon of Xanthan Gum
- 1 Teaspoon of Himalayan Pink Salt
- ½ Cup of crushed Pistachio Nuts

Directions:

1. Preheat your oven to about 325 F.
2. Whisk the eggs in a large mixing bowl until they becomes fluffy.
3. In a separate bowl, melt the almond butter until it becomes soft.
4. Add the butter to a bowl with the sweeteners, the extracts, and the almond milk.
5. Blend your ingredients until it is very well incorporated.
6. Add the Pistachio Extract, the vanilla Extract, the almond Flour, the coconut flour, the baking powder; the Xanthan gum and the salt.
7. Whisk your ingredients until they becomes very well mixed.
8. Add your dry ingredients into a large bowl and mix very we well.
9. Add the crushed pistachios; then fold until it is blended.
10. Grease a muffin tin of about 12 cups or liners.
11. Evenly pour the batter into each of the muffin cups.
12. Bake the muffins for about 25 to 30 minutes.
13. Let your muffins cool for about 5 minutes.
14. Serve and enjoy your muffins!

Nutrition Information

Calories: 198| Fat: 12 g | Carbohydrates: 11g | Fiber: 2g |Protein: 6

Recipe 29: Flax Seed muffins

Preparation time: 8 minutes

Cooking time: 21 minutes

Yield: 12 Servings

Ingredients:

- 1 Cup of ground golden flax seed
- 4 Large Pastured eggs
- ½ Cup of avocado oil or any type of oil
- ½ Cup of swerve
- ¼ Cup of coconut flour
- 2 Teaspoons of vanilla extract
- 2 Teaspoons of cinnamon

- 1 Teaspoon of lemon juice
- ½ Teaspoon of baking soda
- 1 Pinch of sea salt
- 1 Cup of chopped walnuts

Directions:

1. Preheat your oven to a temperature of about 325 F.
2. If the flaxseed is not ground, grind it with a coffee grinder.
3. Mix the flax seeds with the pastured eggs, the avocado oil, the Swerve, the coconut flour, the vanilla extract, the cinnamon, the lemon juice, the baking soda, the salt and the walnuts with an electric mixer.
4. Prepare a muffin pan of 12 holes and line it with silicone muffin cups or parchment paper cups.
5. Distribute the batter evenly between the muffin cups; then bake it for about 18 to 21 minutes at a temperature of 325 F.
6. Serve and enjoy your muffins!

Nutrition Information

Calories: 218| Fat: 20g | Carbohydrates: 6g | Fiber: 3g |Protein: 6.3

Recipe 30: Peanut butter muffins

Preparation time: 8 minutes

Cooking time: 21 minutes

Yield: 12 Servings

Ingredients:

- 1 Cup of almond flour
- ½ Cup of So Nourished erythritol
- 1 Teaspoon of baking powder
- 1 Pinch of salt
- 1/3 Cup of peanut butter
- 1/3 Cup of almond milk
- 2 Large eggs
- ½ Cup of cacao nibs

Directions:

1. Preheat your oven to a temperature of about 350 F.
2. In a large mixing bowl; combine the almond flour with the baking powder, the salt and the erythritol.
3. Add the peanut butter and the almond milk and stir.
4. Add in the eggs, one at a time; then stir until each is fully whisked.
5. Add in the cacao nibs and spray a muffin tin with cooking spray.
6. Evenly distribute the batter between the muffin tins and bake for about 20 to 30 minutes.
7. Remove the muffins from the oven and let cool for 5 minutes.
8. Serve and enjoy your delicious muffins!

Nutrition Information

Calories: 265| Fat: 20.4g | Carbohydrates: 4g | Fiber: 2.7g |Protein: 7.6g

Anna Bright

KETO DESSERTS

Recipe 31: Flourless chocolate cake

Preparation time: 10 minutes

Cooking time: 45 minutes

Yield: 6 Servings

Ingredients:

- ½ Cup of stevia

- 12 Ounces of unsweetened baking chocolate
- 2/3 Cup of ghee
- 1/3 Cup of warm water
- ¼ Teaspoon of salt
- 4 Large pastured eggs
- 2 Cups of boiling water

Directions:

1. Line the bottom of a 9-inch pan of a spring form with a parchment paper.
2. Heat the water in a small pot; then add the salt and the stevia over the water until wait until the mixture becomes completely dissolved.
3. Melt the baking chocolate into a double boiler or simply microwave it for about 30 seconds.
4. Mix the melted chocolate and the butter in a large bowl with an electric mixer.
5. Beat in your hot mixture; then crack in the egg and whisk after adding each of the eggs.
6. Pour the obtained mixture into your prepared spring form tray.
7. Wrap the spring form tray with a foil paper.
8. Place the spring form tray in a large cake tray and add boiling water right to the outside; make sure the depth doesn't exceed 1 inch.
9. Bake the cake into the water bath for about 45 minutes at a temperature of about 350 F.
10. Remove the tray from the boiling water and transfer to a wire to cool.
11. Let the cake chill for an overnight in the refrigerator.
12. Serve and enjoy your delicious cake!

Nutrition Information

Calories: 295| Fat: 26g | Carbohydrates: 6g | Fiber: 4g |Protein: 8g

Recipe 32: Raspberry cake with white chocolate sauce

Preparation time: 15 minutes

Cooking time: 60 minutes

Yield: 5-6 Servings

Ingredients:

- 5 Ounces of melted cacao butter
- 2 Ounces of grass-fed ghee
- ½ Cup of coconut cream
- 1 Cup of green banana flour
- 3 Teaspoons of pure vanilla
- 4 Large eggs
- ½ Cup of as Lakanto Monk Fruit

- 1 Teaspoon of baking powder
- 2 Teaspoons of apple cider vinegar
- 2 Cup of raspberries

For the white chocolate sauce:

- 3 and ½ ounces of cacao butter
- ½ Cup of coconut cream
- 2 Teaspoons of pure vanilla extract
- 1 Pinch of salt

Directions:

1. Preheat your oven to a temperature of about 280 degrees Fahrenheit.
2. Combine the green banana flour with the pure vanilla extract, the baking powder, the coconut cream, the eggs, the cider vinegar and the monk fruit and mix very well.
3. Leave the raspberries aside and line a cake loaf tin with a baking paper .
4. Pour in the batter into the baking tray and scatter the raspberries over the top of the cake.
5. Place the tray in your oven and bake it for about 60 minutes; in the meantime, prepare the sauce by

Directions for sauce:

6. Combine the cacao cream, the vanilla extract, the cacao butter and the salt in a saucepan over a low heat.
7. Mix all your ingredients with a fork to make sure the cacao butter mixes very well with the cream.
8. Remove from the heat and set aside to cool a little bit; but don't let it harden.
9. Drizzle with the chocolate sauce.
10. Scatter the cake with more raspberries.

11. Slice your cake; then serve and enjoy it!

Nutrition Information

Calories: 323| Fat: 31.5g | Carbohydrates: 9.9g | Fiber: 4g |Protein: 5g

Recipe 33: Ketogenic Lava cake

Preparation time: 10 minutes

Cooking time: 10 minutes

Yield: 2 Servings

Ingredients:

- 2 Oz of dark chocolate; you should at least use chocolate of 85% cocoa solids
- 1 Tablespoon of super-fine almond flour
- 2 Oz of unsalted almond butter
- 2 Large eggs

Directions:

1. Heat your oven to a temperature of about 350 Fahrenheit.
2. Grease 2 heat proof ramekins with almond butter.
3. Now, melt the chocolate and the almond butter and stir very well.
4. Beat the eggs very well with a mixer.
5. Add the eggs to the chocolate and the butter mixture and mix very well with almond flour and the swerve; then stir.
6. Pour the dough into 2 ramekins.
7. Bake for about 9 to 10 minutes.
8. Turn the cakes over plates and serve with pomegranate seeds!

Nutrition Information

Calories: 459| Fat: 39g | Carbohydrates: 3.5g | Fiber: 0.8g |Protein: 11.7g

Recipe 34: Ketogenic Cheese Cake

Preparation time: 15 minutes

Cooking time: 50 minutes

Yield: 6 Servings

Ingredients:

For the Almond Flour Cheesecake Crust:

- 2 Cups of Blanched almond flour
- 1/3 Cup of almond Butter
- 3 Tablespoons of Erythritol (powdered or granular)
- 1 Teaspoon of Vanilla extract

For the Keto Cheesecake Filling:

- 32 Oz of softened Cream cheese

- 1 and ¼ cups of powdered erythritol
- 3 Large Eggs
- 1 Tablespoon of Lemon juice
- 1 Teaspoon of Vanilla extract

Directions:

1. Preheat your oven to a temperature of about 350 degrees F.
2. Grease a spring form pan of 9" with cooking spray or just line its bottom with a parchment paper.
3. In order to make the cheesecake rust, stir in the melted butter, the almond flour, the vanilla extract and the erythritol in a large bowl.
4. The dough will get will be a bit crumbly; so press it into the bottom of your prepared tray.
5. Bake for about 12 minutes; then let cool for about 10 minutes.
6. In the meantime, beat the softened cream cheese and the powdered sweetener at a low speed until it becomes smooth.
7. Crack in the eggs and beat them in at a low to medium speed until it becomes fluffy. Make sure to add one a time.
8. Add in the lemon juice and the vanilla extract and mix at a low to medium speed with a mixer.
9. Pour your filling into your pan right on top of the crust. You can use a spatula to smooth the top of the cake.
10. Bake for about 45 to 50 minutes.
11. Remove the baked cheesecake from your oven and run a knife around its edge.
12. Let the cake cool for about 4 hours in the refrigerator.
13. Serve and enjoy your delicious cheese cake!

Nutrition Information

Calories: 325| Fat: 29g | Carbohydrates: 6g | Fiber: 1g |Protein: 7g

Recipe 35: Cake with whipped cream icing

Preparation time: 20 minutes

Cooking time: 25 minutes

Yield: 7 Servings

Ingredients:

- ¾ Cup Coconut flour
- ¾ Cup of Swerve Sweetener
- ½ Cup of Cocoa powder
- 2 Teaspoons of Baking powder
- 6 Large Eggs
- 2/3 Cup of Heavy Whipping Cream
- ½ Cup of Melted almond Butter

For the whipped Cream Icing:

- 1 Cup of Heavy Whipping Cream
- ¼ Cup of Swerve Sweetener
- 1 Teaspoon of Vanilla extract
- 1/3 Cup of Sifted Cocoa Powder

Directions:

1. Pre-heat your oven to a temperature of about 350 F.
2. Grease an 8x8 cake tray with cooking spray.
3. Add the coconut flour, the Swerve sweetener; the cocoa powder, the baking powder, the eggs, the melted butter; and combine very well with an electric or a hand mixer.
4. Pour your batter into the cake tray and bake for about 25 minutes.
5. Remove the cake tray from the oven and let cool for about 5 minutes.

For the Icing

6. Whip the cream until it becomes fluffy; then add in the Swerve, the vanilla and the cocoa powder.
7. Add the Swerve, the vanilla and the cocoa powder; then continue mixing until your ingredients are very well combined.
8. Frost your baked cake with the icing; then slice it; serve and enjoy your delicious cake!

Nutrition Information

Calories: 357| Fat: 33g | Carbohydrates: 11g | Fiber: 2g |Protein: 8g

Recipe 36: Walnut-Fruit cake

Preparation time: 15 minutes

Cooking time: 20 minutes

Yield: 6 Servings

Ingredients:

- 1/2 Cup of almond butter (softened)
- ¼ Cup of so Nourished granulated erythritol
- 1 Tablespoon of ground cinnamon
- ½ Teaspoon of ground nutmeg
- ¼ Teaspoon of ground cloves
- 4 Large pastured eggs
- 1 Teaspoon of vanilla extract
- ½ Teaspoon of almond extract

- 2 Cups of almond flour
- ½ Cup of chopped walnuts
- ¼ Cup of dried of unsweetened cranberries
- ¼ Cup of seedless raisins

Directions:

1. Preheat your oven to a temperature of about 350 F and grease an 8-inch baking tin of round shape with coconut oil.
2. Beat the granulated erythritol on a high speed until it becomes fluffy.
3. Add the cinnamon, the nutmeg, and the cloves; then blend your ingredients until they become smooth.
4. Crack in the eggs and beat very well by adding one at a time, plus the almond extract and the vanilla.
5. Whisk in the almond flour until it forms a smooth batter then fold in the nuts and the fruit.
6. Spread your mixture into your prepared baking pan and bake it for about 20 minutes.
7. Remove the cake from the oven and let cool for about 5 minutes.
8. Dust the cake with the powdered erythritol.
9. Serve and enjoy your cake!

Nutrition Information

Calories: 250| Fat: 11g | Carbohydrates: 12g | Fiber: 2g |Protein: 7g

Recipe 37: Ginger cake

Preparation time: 15 minutes

Cooking time: 20 minutes

Yield: 9 Servings

Ingredients:

- ½ Tablespoon of unsalted almond butter to grease the pan
- 4 Large eggs
- ¼ Cup coconut milk
- 2 Tablespoons of unsalted almond butter
- 1 and ½ teaspoons of stevia
- 1 Tablespoon of ground cinnamon
- 1 Tablespoon of natural unweeded cocoa powder

- 1 Tablespoon of fresh ground ginger
- ½ Teaspoon of kosher salt
- 1 and ½ cups of blanched almond flour
- ½ Teaspoon of baking soda

Directions:

1. Preheat your oven to a temperature of 325 F.
2. Grease a glass baking tray of about 8X8 inches generously with almond butter.
3. In a large bowl, whisk all together the coconut milk, the eggs, the melted almond butter, the stevia, the cinnamon, the cocoa powder, the ginger and the kosher salt.
4. Whisk in the almond flour, then the baking soda and mix very well.
5. Pour the batter into the prepared pan and bake for about 20 to 25 minutes.
6. Let the cake cool for about 5 minutes; then slice; serve and enjoy your delicious cake.

Nutrition Information

Calories: 175| Fat: 15g | Carbohydrates: 5g | Fiber: 1.9g |Protein: 5g

Recipe 38: Ketogenic orange Cake

Preparation time: 10 minutes

Cooking time: 50minutes

Yield: 8 Servings

Ingredients:

- 2 and ½ cups of almond flour
- 2 Unwaxed washed oranges
- 5 Large separated eggs
- 1 Teaspoon of baking powder
- 2 Teaspoons of orange extract
- 1 Teaspoon of vanilla bean powder
- 6 Seeds of cardamom pods crushed
- 16 drops of liquid stevia; about 3 teaspoons
- 1 Handful of flaked almonds to decorate

Directions:

1. Preheat your oven to a temperature of about 350 Fahrenheit.
2. Line a rectangular bread baking tray with a parchment paper.
3. Place the oranges into a pan filled with cold water and cover it with a lid.
4. Bring the saucepan to a boil, then let simmer for about 1 hour and make sure the oranges are totally submerged.
5. Make sure the oranges are always submerged to remove any taste of bitterness.
6. Cut the oranges into halves; then remove any seeds; and drain the water and set the oranges aside to cool down.
7. Cut the oranges in half and remove any seeds, then puree it with a blender or a food processor.
8. Separate the eggs; then whisk the egg whites until you see stiff peaks forming.
9. Add all your ingredients except for the egg whites to the orange mixture and add in the egg whites; then mix.
10. Pour the batter into the cake tin and sprinkle with the flaked almonds right on top.
11. Bake your cake for about 50 minutes.
12. Remove the cake from the oven and set aside to cool for 5 minutes.
13. Slice your cake; then serve and enjoy its incredible taste!

Nutrition Information

Calories: 164| Fat: 12g | Carbohydrates: 7.1 | Fiber: 2.7g |Protein: 10.9g

Recipe 39: Lemon cake

Preparation time: 20 minutes

Cooking time: 20minutes

Yield: 9 Servings

Ingredients:

- 2 Medium lemons
- 4 Large eggs
- 2 Tablespoons of almond butter
- 2 Tablespoons of avocado oil
- 1/3 cup of coconut flour
- 4-5 tablespoons of honey (or another sweetener of your choice)
- ½ tablespoon of baking soda

Directions:

1. Preheat your oven to a temperature of about 350 F.
2. Crack the eggs in a large bowl and set two egg whites aside.
3. Whisk the 2 whites of eggs with the egg yolks, the honey, the oil, the almond butter, the lemon zest and the juice and whisk very well together.
4. Combine the baking soda with the coconut flour and gradually add this dry mixture to the wet ingredients and keep whisking for a couple of minutes.
5. Beat the two eggs with a hand mixer and beat the egg into foam.
6. Add the white egg foam gradually to the mixture with a silicone spatula.
7. Transfer your obtained batter to tray covered with a baking paper.
8. Bake your cake for about 20 to 22 minutes.
9. Let the cake cool for 5 minutes; then slice your cake.
10. Serve and enjoy your delicious cake!

Nutrition Information

Calories: 164| Fat: 12g | Carbohydrates: 7.1 | Fiber: 2.7g |Protein: 10.9g

Recipe 40: Cinnamon cake

Preparation time: 15 minutes

Cooking time: 35minutes

Yield: 8 Servings

Ingredients

For the Cinnamon Filling:

- 3 Tablespoons of Swerve Sweetener
- 2 Teaspoons of ground cinnamon

For the Cake:
- 3 Cups of almond flour
- ¾ Cup of Swerve Sweetener

- ¼ Cup of unflavoured whey protein powder
- 2 Teaspoon of baking powder
- ½ Teaspoon of salt
- 3 large pastured eggs
- ½ Cup of melted coconut oil
- ½ Teaspoon of vanilla extract
- ½ Cup of almond milk
- 1 Tablespoon of melted coconut oil

For the cream cheese Frosting:

- 3 Tablespoons of softened cream cheese
- 2 Tablespoons of powdered Swerve Sweetener
- 1 Tablespoon of coconut heavy whipping cream
- ½ Teaspoon of vanilla extract

Directions:

1. Preheat your oven to a temperature of about 325 F and grease a baking tray of 8x8 inch.
2. For the filling, mix the Swerve and the cinnamon in a mixing bowl and mix very well; then set it aside.
3. For the preparation of the cake; whisk all together the almond flour, the sweetener, the protein powder, the baking powder, and the salt in a mixing bowl.
4. Add in the eggs, the melted coconut oil and the vanilla extract and mix very well.
5. Add in the almond milk and keep stirring until your ingredients are very well combined.
6. Spread about half of the batter in the prepared pan; then sprinkle with about two thirds of the filling mixture.
7. Spread the remaining mixture of the batter over the filling and smooth it with a spatula.
8. Bake for about 35 minutes in the oven.

9. Brush with the melted coconut oil and sprinkle with the remaining cinnamon filling.
10. Prepare the frosting by beating the cream cheese, the powdered erythritol, the cream and the vanilla extract in a mixing bowl until it becomes smooth.
11. Drizzle frost over the cooled cake.
12. Slice the cake; then serve and enjoy your cake!

Nutrition Information

Calories: 222| Fat: 19.2g | Carbohydrates: 5.4g | Fiber: 1.5g |Protein: 7.3g

Anna Bright

KETO SNACKS AND TREATS

Recipe 41: Ketogenic Madeleine

Preparation time: 10 minutes

Cooking time: 15 minutes

Yield: 12 Servings

Ingredients

- 2 Large pastured eggs
- ¾ Cup of almond flour
- 1 and ½ Tablespoons of Swerve
- ¼ Cup of cooled, melted coconut oil
- 1 Teaspoon of vanilla extract
- 1 Teaspoon of almond extract
- 1 Teaspoon of lemon zest
- ¼ Teaspoon of salt

Directions

1. Preheat your oven to a temperature of about 350 F.
2. Combine the eggs with the salt and whisk on a high speed for about 5 minutes.
3. Slowly add in the Swerve and keep mixing on high for 2 additional minutes.
4. Stir in the almond flour until it is very well-incorporated; then add in the vanilla and the almond extracts.
5. Add in the melted coconut oil and stir all your ingredients together.
6. Pour the obtained batter into equal parts in a greased Madeleine tray.

7. Bake your Ketogenic Madeleine for about 13 minutes or until the edges start to have a brown color.
8. Flip the Madeleines out of the baking tray.
9. Serve and enjoy your madeleines!

Nutrition Information

Calories: 87| Fat: 8.1g | Carbohydrates: 3g | Fiber: 2g |Protein: 8g

Recipe 42: Keto Waffles

Preparation time: 20 minutes

Cooking time: 30 minutes

Yield: 3 Servings

Ingredients:

For the Ketogenic waffles:

- 8 Oz of cream cheese
- 5 Large pastured eggs
- 1/3 Cup of coconut flour
- ½ Teaspoon of Xanthan gum
- 1 Pinch of salt
- ½ Teaspoon of vanilla extract

- 2 Tablespoons of Swerve
- ¼ Teaspoon of baking soda
- 1/3 Cup of almond milk

Optional ingredients:

- ½ Teaspoon of cinnamon pie spice
- ¼ Teaspoon of almond extract

To prepare the low-carb Maple Syrup:
- 1 Cup of water
- 1 Tablespoon of Maple flavour
- ¾ Cup of powdered Swerve
- 1 Tablespoon of almond butter
- ½ Teaspoon of Xanthan gum

Directions

For the waffles:
1. Make sure all your ingredients are exactly at room temperature.
2. Place all your ingredients for the waffles from cream cheese to pastured eggs, coconut flour, Xanthan gum, salt, vanilla extract, the Swerve, the baking soda and the almond milk except for the almond milk with the help of a processor.
3. Blend your ingredients until it becomes smooth and creamy; then transfer the batter to a bowl.
4. Add the almond milk and mix your ingredients with a spatula.
5. Heat a waffle maker to a temperature of high.
6. Spray your waffle maker with coconut oil and add about ¼ of the batter in it evenly with a spatula into your waffle iron.

7. Close your waffle and cook until you get the colour you want.
8. Carefully remove the waffles to a platter.

For the Ketogenic Maple Syrup:
9. Place 1 and ¼ cups of water, the swerve and the maple in a small pan and bring to a boil over a low heat; then let simmer for about 10 minutes.
10. Add the coconut oil.
11. Sprinkle the Xanthan gum over the top of the waffle and use an immersion blender to blend smoothly.
12. Serve and enjoy your delicious waffles!

Nutrition Information

Calories: 316| Fat: 26g | Carbohydrates: 7g | Fiber: 3g |Protein: 11g

Recipe 43: Ketogenic pretzels

Preparation time: 10 minutes

Cooking time: 20 minutes

Yield: 7-8 Servings

Ingredients:

- 1 and ½ cups of pre-shredded mozzarella
- 2 Tablespoons of full fat cream cheese
- 1 Large egg
- ¾ Cup of almond flour+ 2 tablespoons of ground almonds or almond meal
- ½ Teaspoon of baking powder
- 1 Pinch of coarse sea salt

Directions:

1. Heat your oven to a temperature of about 180 C/356 F.
2. Melt the cream cheese and the mozzarella cheese and stir over a low heat until the cheeses are perfectly melted.
3. If you choose to microwave the cheese, just do that for about 1 minute no more and if you want to do it on the stove, turn off the heat as soon as the cheese is completely melted.
4. Add the large egg to the prepared warm dough; then stir until your ingredients are very well combined. If the egg is cold; you will need to gently heat it.
5. Add in the ground almonds or the almond flour and the baking powder and stir until your ingredients are very well combined.
6. Take one pinch of the dough of cheese and toll it or stretch it in your hands until it is about 18 to 20 cm of length; if your dough is sticky, you can oil your hands to avoid that.
7. Now, form pretzels from the cheese dough and nicely shape it; then place it over a baking sheet.
8. Sprinkle with a little bit of salt and bake for about 17 minutes.
9. Serve and enjoy your pretzels!

Nutrition Information

Calories: 113| Fat: 8.4g | Carbohydrates: 2.5g | Fiber: 0.8g |Protein: 8.7g

Recipe 44: Cheesy Taco bites

Preparation time: 5 minutes

Cooking time: 10minutes

Yield: 12 Servings

Ingredients

- 2 Cups of Packaged Shredded Cheddar Cheese
- 2 Tablespoon of Chilli Powder
- 2 Tablespoons of Cumin
- 1 Teaspoon of Salt
- 8 Teaspoons of coconut cream for garnishing
- Use Pico de Gallo for garnishing as well

Directions:

1. Preheat your oven to a temperature of about 350 F.
2. Over a baking sheet lined with a parchment paper, place 1 tablespoon piles of cheese and make sure to a space of 2 inches between each.
3. Place the baking sheet in your oven and bake for about 5 minutes.
4. Remove from the oven and let the cheese cool down for about 1 minute; then carefully lift up and press each into the cups of a mini muffin tin.
5. Make sure to press the edges of the cheese to form the shape of muffins mini.
6. Let the cheese cool completely; then remove it.
7. While you continue to bake the cheese and create your cups.
8. Fill the cheese cups with the coconut cream, then top with the Pico de Gallo.
9. Serve and enjoy your delicious snack!

Nutrition Information

Calories: 73| Fat: 5g | Carbohydrates: 3g | Fiber: 1g |Protein: 4g

Recipe 45: Nut squares

Preparation time: 30 minutes

Cooking time: 10 minutes

Yield: 10 Servings

Ingredients:

- 2 Cups of almonds, pumpkin seeds, sunflower seeds and walnuts
- ½ Cup of desiccated coconut
- 1 Tablespoon of chia seeds
- ¼ Teaspoon of salt
- 2 Tablespoons of coconut oil
- 1 Teaspoon of vanilla extract
- 3 Tablespoons of almond or peanut butter
- 1/3 Cup of Sukrin Gold Fiber Syrup

Directions:

1. Line a square baking tin with a baking paper; then lightly grease it with cooking spray
2. Chop all the nuts roughly; then slightly grease it too, you can also leave them as whole
3. Mix the nuts in a large bowl; then combine them in a large bowl with the coconut, the chia seeds and the salt
4. In a microwave-proof bowl; add the coconut oil; then add the vanilla, the coconut butter or oil, the almond butter and the fiber syrup and microwave the mixture for about 30 seconds
5. Stir your ingredients together very well; then pour the melted mixture right on top of the nuts
6. Press the mixture into your prepared baking tin with the help of the back of a measuring cup and push very well
7. Freeze your treat for about 1 hour before cutting it
8. Cut your frozen nut batter into small cubes or squares of the same size
9. Serve and enjoy!

Nutrition Information

Calories: 268| Fat: 22g | Carbohydrates: 14g | Fiber: 1g |Protein: 7g

Recipe 46: Coconut snack bars

Preparation time: 30 minutes

Cooking time: 0 minutes

Yield: 13 Servings

Ingredients:

- 2Cups of coconut flakes
- ¾ Cup of melted coconut oil
- 1 and ½ cups of macadamia nuts
- 1 large scoop of vanilla protein powder
- ¼ Cup of unsweetened dark chocolate chips

Directions:

1. Gather the coconut flakes with the melted coconut oil, the macadamia nuts, the vanilla protein powder and the dark chocolate chips in a large bowl and mix very well.
2. Line an 8×8 baking tray with a parchment paper.
3. Process the macadamia nuts with the coconut oil in a food processor until it becomes smooth.
4. Pour the batter into a pan and freeze it for about 30 minutes.
5. Cut the frozen batter into bars with a sharp knife into your preferred size.
6. Serve and enjoy your Ketogenic treat or store it and serve it whenever you want.

Nutrition Information

Calories: 213.7| Fat: 20g | Carbohydrates: 6g | Fiber: 2 g |Protein: 4g

Recipe 47: Flax seed Crackers

Preparation time: 8 minutes

Cooking time: 10 minutes

Yield: 25 Servings

Ingredients:

- 2 and 1/2 cups of almond flour
- ½ Cup of coconut flour
- 1 Teaspoon of ground flaxseed meal
- ½ Teaspoon of dried rosemary, chopped
- ½ Teaspoon of onion powder
- ¼ Teaspoon of kosher salt
- 3 large organic eggs
- 1 Tablespoon of extra-virgin olive oil

Directions:

1. Preheat your oven to a temperature of about 325 F.
2. Line a baking sheet with a parchment paper.
3. In a large bowl; combine the flours with the rosemary, the flax meal, the salt and the onion powder and mix.
4. Crack in the eggs and add the oil; then mix very well and combine your ingredients very well.
5. Keep mixing until you get the shape of a large ball for about 1 minute.
6. Cut the dough into the 2 pieces of parchment paper and roll it to a thickness of about ¼".
7. Cut the dough into squares and transfer it to the prepared baking sheet.
8. Bake your dough for about 13 to 15 minutes; then let cool for about 15 minutes.
9. Serve and enjoy your crackers or store in a container.

Nutrition Information

Calories: 150.2| Fat: 13g | Carbohydrates: 5.4g | Fiber: 2.6g |Protein: 7g

Recipe 48: Almond flour crackers

Preparation time: 7 minutes

Cooking time: 12 minutes

Yield: 15 Servings

Ingredients:

- 2 Cups of Blanched almond flour
- ½ Teaspoon of sea salt
- 1 Beaten large Egg

Directions:

1. Preheat your oven to a temperature of about 350 F .
2. Line a baking sheet with a parchment paper; then combine the almond flour and the salt in a large bowl;

then crack in the egg and mix very well until you form a large ball of dough.
3. Place your dough between two large pieces of prepared parchment paper; then use a rolling pin to roll the dough into a rectangular shape.
4. Cut the dough into rectangles; then prick it with a fork and place it over the prepared and lined baking sheet.
5. Bake your crackers for about 8 to 12 minutes.
6. Let the crackers cool for about 10 minutes.
7. Store the crackers in a container; or serve and enjoy them right away!

Nutrition Information

Calories: 120| Fat: 6g | Carbohydrates: 14g | Fiber: 2g |Protein: 3g

Recipe 49: Keto sugar free candies

Preparation time: 30 minutes

Cooking time: 0 minutes

Yield: 12 Servings

Ingredients:

- 4 Oz of Coconut Oil, melted
- 4.5 Oz of Shredded, unsweetened Coconut
- 1 Teaspoon of Stevia
- 3 Oz of Erythritol powder
- 1 Large egg white
- 1 Teaspoon of vanilla extract
- 3 Drops of Red Food Colouring

- ½ Teaspoon of Strawberry Extract

Directions:

1. In a large bowl, mix all together the erythritol, the shredded coconut, the stevia and the vanilla with a hand blender on a low heat.
2. Melt the coconut oil in a small saucepan over a low heat.
3. Add the oil to the shredded coconut mixture and combine very well.
4. Add in the egg white and mix; then combine half of the mixture into a square dish of about 8 squares and set it aside.
5. Add the strawberry essence and the food colouring and strawberry essence to the remaining mixture and mix very well.
6. Press the mixture right top of the white mixture into the square dish and set it aside in the fridge for about 1 hour.
7. When your coconut ice is perfectly set, cut it into 16 pieces.
8. Serve and enjoy!

Nutrition Information

Calories: 119| Fat: 12g | Carbohydrates: 2g | Fiber: 1g |Protein: 3g

Recipe 50: Keto donuts

Preparation time: 5 minutes

Cooking time: 0 minutes

Yield: 4 Servings

Ingredients:

For the donut ingredients:

- ½ Cup of sifted almond flour
- 3 to 4 tablespoons of coconut milk
- 2 Large eggs
- 2 to 3 tablespoons granulated of stevia
- 1 Teaspoon of Keto-friendly baking powder

- 1 Heap teaspoon of apple cider vinegar
- 1 Pinch of salt
- 1 and ½ Tablespoon of sifted cacao powder
- 3 Teaspoons of Ceylon cinnamon
- 1 Teaspoon of powdered vanilla bean
- 1 Tablespoon of grass-fed ghee
- 2 Tablespoons of Coconut oil for greasing

For the Icing Ingredients:

- 4 Tablespoons of melted coconut butter with 1 to 2 teaspoons of coconut oil
- Optional garnishing ingredients: edible rose petals, or shredded cacao

Directions:

1. Preheat the oven to a temperature of about 350 degrees.
2. Grease a donut tray with the coconut oil.
3. Stir all together the sifted almond flour with the coconut milk, eggs, the granulated of stevia, the Keto-friendly baking powder, the apple cider vinegar, the salt, the sifted cocoa powder, the Ceylon cinnamon, the powdered vanilla bean and the grass-fed ghee.
4. Mix your donut ingredients until they are evenly combined.
5. Divide the obtained batter into the donut moulds making sure to fill each to ¾ full.
6. Bake for about 8 minutes; then remove the tray from the oven and carefully transfer it to a wire rack.
7. Serve and enjoy your donut or top it with the icing and the garnish of your choice.
8. Serve and enjoy your delicious treat!

Nutrition Information

Calories: 122| Fat: 6.8g | Carbohydrates: 13.5g | Fiber: 2.3g |Protein: 3g

KETO SMOOTHIE, ICE CREAM, MOUSSE, MILKSHAKE, PUDDING

Recipe 51: Coconut milk Pear Shake

Preparation time: 2 minutes

Cooking time: 0 minutes

Yield: 3-4 Servings

Ingredients:

- 4 Ripe chopped pears
- 4 lettuce leaves finely torn into pieces
- ¼ Cup of unsweetened coconut milk
- 5 Dried and toasted Almonds
- 4 Leaves of mint
- 2 Tablespoons of unsweetened orange juice
- ½ Tablespoon of apple sauce
- 5 ice cubes

Direction

1. Place the chopped pears in the blender.
2. Add the lettuce leaves.
3. Pour in the almond milk and the rest of the ingredients with the ice cubes.
4. Blend all of your ingredients for around 3 minutes.
5. Serve and enjoy!

Nutrition Information

Calories: 60| Fat: 3g | Carbohydrates: 2.8g | Fiber: 1g |Protein: 3g

Recipe 52: Chocolate Pudding

Preparation time: 5 minutes

Cooking time: 0 minutes

Yield: 3 Servings

Ingredients:

- 1 Avocado
- ¼ Cup of apple sauce
- ¼ Cup of organic raw unsweetened cacao powder
- 2 Organic Medjool dates
- 1 Tablespoon of organic coconut oil
- 1 Tablespoon of homemade almond milk

For the crust:

- 1 Cup of organic walnuts
- 2 Organic Medjool dates
- 2 Tablespoons of organic raw cacao powder
- 1 Tablespoon of coconut oil

Directions

1. Start by preparing the crust.
2. Add all of your ingredients into a food processor and then process it until you obtain a sticky mixture.
3. Divide your mixture into halves and then press it into the bottom of 2 cavities of tart moulds and set it aside.
4. Prepare your pudding by combining all of your ingredients into a blender and keep blending until you obtain a creamy mixture.
5. Transfer your smooth mixture to the mould you have prepared on the crust and make sure to spread it evenly.
6. Top with pistachios, walnuts, raw cacao nibs or hemp seeds.
7. Serve and enjoy!

Nutrition Information

Calories: 227| Fat: 22g | Carbohydrates: 12g | Fiber: 3g |Protein: 3.5g

Recipe 53: Raspberry smoothie

Preparation time: 5 minutes

Cooking time: 0 minutes

Yield: 3 Servings

Ingredients

- 1 Cup of water
- 2 Cups of chopped lettuce
- 1 Cup of fresh or frozen raspberries
- 1 Tablespoon of flax seeds
- 1 Teaspoon of chia seeds
- A little bit of unsweetened apple sauce
- 1 Teaspoon of coconut oil

Directions

1. Place your ingredients into your blender.
2. Blend your ingredients at high speed for around 1 minute.
3. Check on the thickness of the smoothie, if it is creamy and smooth, serve and enjoy!

Recipe 54: Cocoa Mousse

Preparation time: 3 minutes

Cooking time: 0 minutes

Yield: 2 Servings

Ingredients

- 1 Cup of Heavy Whipping coconut Cream
- ¼ Cup of sifted, unsweetened cocoa powder
- ¼ Cup of Swerve
- 1 Teaspoon of Vanilla extract
- ¼ Teaspoon of kosher salt

Directions:

1. Start by whisking the cream until it starts stiffening.
2. Add in the stevia, the vanilla and the salt and whisk your ingredients very well.
3. Add the cocoa powder to your ingredients and whisk again.
4. Serve and enjoy your Cocoa mousse!

Nutrition Information

Calories: 218| Fat: 23g | Carbohydrates: 5g | Fiber: 1 g |Protein: 3g

Recipe 55: Coconut Ice Cream

Preparation time: 3 minutes

Cooking time: 0 minutes

Yield: 2 Servings

Ingredients:

- 2 Cups of canned coconut milk
- 1/3 Cup of stevia
- 1/8 Teaspoon of salt
- 1 1/2 tsp pure vanilla extract or vanilla bean paste
- optional ingredients for desired flavour

Directions:

1. Make sure to use full-fat canned coconut milk.

2. You can also use the seeds of a vanilla bean instead of the extract.
3. Now, to make the ice cream, mix the milk with the Swerve the salt and the vanilla extract.
4. If you own an ice cream machine, you can simply churn by following the manufacturer's instructions.
5. Freeze the obtained mixture into ice cube trays then blend in a blender on a high-speed; you can use a Vitamix for example.
6. Freeze the ice cream for about 30 minutes.
7. Serve and enjoy your ice cream!

Nutrition Information

Calories: 283| Fat: 21.5g | Carbohydrates: 5.1g | Fiber: 1.3 g |Protein: 3.2g

CONCLUSION

Sticking to a specific diet like the Ketogenic diet has proven to be an effective way to help us get into shape and lose weight. Combined with some exercises, the Ketogenic diet has shown great results for many people who had lost hope of losing weight and who used to suffer serious health conditions before adopting the Ketogenic diet. Not only can the Ketogenic diet help you to maintain great health, but it can also improve your energy, stamina and will incredibly boost the activity of your immunity system.

But while the Ketogenic diet has shown the greatest results as far as health and weight are concerned, this diet can be quite frustrating for many people as it prevents them from enjoying some of their most favourite foods like bread and desserts. However, after reading this cookbook, you will discover that this idea is completely wrong and you will find out that even on a Ketogenic diet, you can still enjoy eating your favourite sorts of bread and even desserts.

So, if you are new to the Ketogenic diet and you are reluctant whether to adopt it or not, don't hesitate anymore because this diet will help you enjoy some of your favourite recipes in a new style and way. While it is true that adopting the Ketogenic diet will change your life forever, it is not a scary diet that you imagine it is. You can still enjoy the mesmerising tastes of delicious types of food, breads and even desserts by using completely healthy ingredients. Thus, adopting a Ketogenic diet will not only help you lose weight, but it will also lead you to live a longer and healthier life.

With this book, you will learn that adopting the Ketogenic diet cannot be easier; and all that you have to do is to use an array of healthy ingredients. While you are willing to adopt the Ketogenic diet, you should first read the introductory chapters that explain everything about this diet and that offers you many details you should know about this diet before adopting it as your new diet and lifestyle. Not only will the Ketogenic diet make your life change for better, but it will also help you enjoy cooking and eating food the way you never did before. You will also discover that the dietary lifestyles have progressed so much in a way that can offer you guilt free tastes you are looking for. Guess what, you won't be counting carbohydrates from now on, because in this cookbook, you will find each recipe with already calculated nutrition information.

Most of the recipes you will find in this book are easy-to make with simple-to follow instructions for you and your adorable family, friends or even for your own sake. You will even feel better after consuming the incredible and sumptuous 55 Ketogenic bread and dessert recipes that you will find in this book. So, are you ready to get started? If yes, then let's do it!

Thank you for Reading This Book Entitled

"Keto Bread and Desserts"

I am glad that I have offered you this Ketogenic diet cook book and I take pride in offering you some of the most delicious recipes you can ever taste or enjoy. This cookbook would have never been able come to existence without your help dear readers and without your encouragement. You are my inspiration, and I could have never have felt happier. I hope that you will benefit from this book and enjoy it as much as you can. I encourage you to share this Keto diet cookbook with your friends and they won't regret it!